INTRODUCTION

This book is about autism, to create awareness and understanding of the mind and idiosyncrasies of autistic people and all who struggle to fit in.

This book is about autism, to appreciate the wonders of seeing the world differently and the beauty of these differences.

This book is about autism, to bring the much needed recognition and help that leads to hope and joy and growth.

NOTE: This book was created with love and care by a team of writers and artists who have friends and family on the autism spectrum.

CHAPTER ONE / MEET MATTY

In a world far tinier than what we humans know

There lived a special gray mouse named Matty.

Matty was different. He was very well aware of that. You see, he had a unique way of seeing and experiencing the world as if he wore magical glasses that painted the world in brilliant colors.

Matty loved his special glasses,

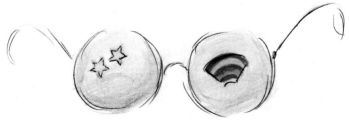

But it seemed no one else had special glasses. His family didn't have them. They were different, they talked differently, they smelled differently, and they even looked different. His mom, dad, sisters, and everyone he knew, **were bats.**

Being a mouse in a family of bats wasn't all bad. Matty couldn't imagine it any other way. Yet, sometimes, he wished that they understood him just a tiny bit better.

For Example

Every school morning, after breakfast, his sisters Lira and Sira
would soar through the sky without effort to get to school.

Matty dreamed he could too.

But, Matty could not fly like a bat. He had to run along on the ground.

It took him so much longer because he couldn't take the bat route through the air, dancing with the wind. And to top it all off, he could not talk with the other kids about how cool the cloud formations looked.

He had asked Lira and Sira a trillion times to tell him about the clouds, but they kept it a secret. How often did he wish his family could see his struggles and be patient with him?

He hoped that maybe one day, he would grow his own wings. Who knew?

Weekends

Matty whined when his mom walked into his room to kiss him goodnight.

"But aren't you excited, Matty? She responded in a comforting way.

"Tomorrow you'll have sports in the afternoon. I used to love sports when I was your age!"

"No, mom," he said, shaking his head firmly. "Watching the others do flying dance is not fun."

"I'm sure you'll have a good time anyway, sweetheart," she said, turning off the lights.

What his mom didn't know

Matty could not tell her that he felt stupid trying to do the flying dance with no wings.

He had a big bubble of worries around his head because the other kids made fun of him every day.

It was lonely, especially in school. He wanted friends.

In his dream, he had wings like the others, finally feeling like he belonged and fit in.

"Will I ever be normal, like a bat?" he wondered.

At breakfast

Lira and Sira couldn't wait to fly to school and talked loudly about a flying exam they had today.

Matty didn't listen. The only thing he could think about was how much he didn't want to attend school. He poked listlessly in his raspberry and bugs cereal.

"Why the sad face, Matty?" his Dad asked gently.

A thousand reasons ran through his mind, but "tired" was the only thing he mumbled.

Meanwhile, Sira and Lira flew through the air with a fantastic view of thick fluffy clouds. They were the popular twins who liked being at school and were perfect at performing flying tricks, while their weird little brother was misunderstood by everyone, including his own parents.

Matty had to hurry and run through bushes, stones, and sticky moss, all to get to a place he didn't even want to be. A place filled with mean kids who didn't have magical glasses.

Wasn't it totally unfair?

CHAPTER TWO/MEET PORTOS

Matty was already late and anxious as he ran toward the famous "Bats' School Cave." The school was surrounded by green bushes and white flowers.

As he ran past the bushes, thinking about his nightmare coming closer, he stumbled upon a huge and hairy creature.

Argggh, Matty screamed.

Never in his life had he seen such a wondrous-looking thing.

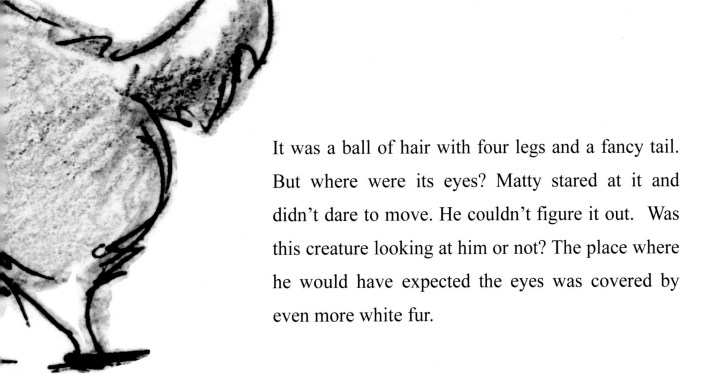

It was a ball of hair with four legs and a fancy tail. But where were its eyes? Matty stared at it and didn't dare to move. He couldn't figure it out. Was this creature looking at him or not? The place where he would have expected the eyes was covered by even more white fur.

"Woof" the creature said...

Matty stared in awe. "What in the world are you?" he asked.

"I'm Portos," the creature announced. "Why the angry face, mouse?" he asked with a friendly voice.

Little did Matty know that this creature named Portos had seen many things in his long life and had a great understanding of the world.

"Oh, young mouse, do you feel different in school?" Portos asked gently, then he explained.

"Being different isn't all bad and thunder. It makes you somewhat special. It's a gift!"

Matty couldn't understand why Portos said it was a gift to be different, it didn't feel like it at all...

Matty sighed and wondered, "Did Portos have magical glasses under all that fur?" He wanted to talk more with Portos, but...

The Bats School bell rang.

He hurried into the cave to get to class in time,

but his classroom was so deep in the cave

that it took him way too long.

At Bats School Matty felt so ashamed, as he made his way to his spot. The eyes of twenty young bats stared at him. He couldn't find the words to explain why he was late. He often struggled to find the right words.

Undoubtedly, the others must have thought
he was late because he couldn't fly.

They often called him **"wingless weirdo".** No matter how
hard he tried to fit in, he couldn't connect with them.

During snack time

Matty wanted to appear like a normal boy bat, pretending not to have any worries.

Be like a bat!

Act like a bat!

He told himself, but he was sure he didn't fool anyone.

A fat walnut of sadness was sitting in his belly today.

But he couldn't even have a snack because it was too far up.

Matty cried inside, "I can't fool anyone. The other
kids are cooler. Will they ever be nice to me?

I'm weird. I'm stupid."

CHAPTER THREE / DAY DREAMING

The only thing that brought Matty joy and distracted him

wa*s* **daydreaming** about his favorite topic...

finding interesting images on old leaves.

Lost in his thoughts and dreams, **he was calm and happy.**

He often wondered if the reason he dreamed his way through the day, imagining leaves with faces and birds and flowers on them, was because of his magical glasses. The others didn't seem to be able to see the world the same way he did. They didn't have magical glasses.

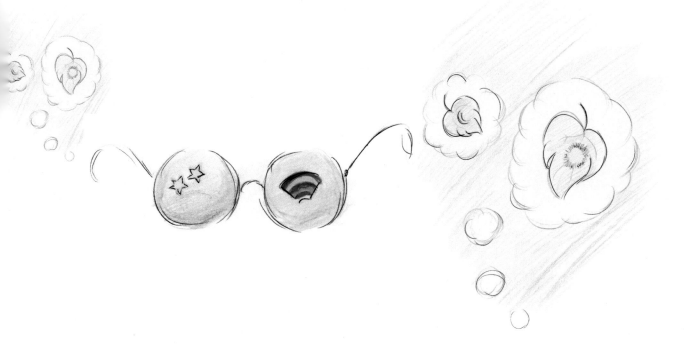

Last fall, he had found a leaf with a sunny, happy face on it, but when he proudly showed his classmates, they burst into mean laughter.

Because, for them, it was just an old uninteresting leaf.

Ever since that day, he kept his discoveries to himself.

As Matty dreamed, **the trees spoke to him**.

"Being different makes you unique, Matty,"

whispered the tall oak in a deep, comforting voice.

"It's a gift," the bushes chanted from all around.

"You have the magical glasses," howled the wind.

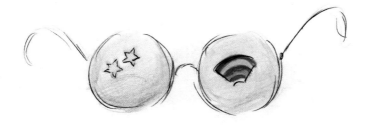

"You are special," sang the young maple.

The forest spoke to him again and again.

Matty began to feel joy inside.

When Matty opened his eyes

His keen senses could hear his parents in the kitchen, cooking.

His nose quickly detected the smell of his dad's fresh fruit pie.

Something was different. His belly felt lighter.

He felt happier, not so grumpy...

…until his sisters, Sira and Lira started to laugh,

"haha, silly Matty, we saw you daydreaming under trees in the schoolyard."

Mean twins…

Matty's happiness disappeared like a magic trick.

He didn't want to tell his family about his daydreams,

or about bumping into that weird, hairy creature.

Matty crawled inside of himself.

CHAPTER FOUR / PORTOS, OH PORTOS

Matty wondered if he would ever run into Portos again.

Portos was the first one who ever told him

he was good just the way he was.

When little Matty finally got on his way to school,

all he could think about was **would he see Portos again**

As he ran through the forest, a funny whistling melody tickled his ears.
What is that? He wondered as he stopped right in front of a gigantic oak tree.

The whistling turned into happy giggling.

Matty scratched his head and pondered for a moment
whether to ignore it, or follow the mysterious sound.

Curiosity won.

His huge floppy ears, with their high sensory power, perked up.

The whistling and giggling sounds came from inside the old oak tree.

Sniff, sniff.

He tested the air, searching for a scent.

Sniff, sniff.

A slight whiff of freshly dug soil and
something sweet and fruity tickled his nose.

Sniff, sniff.

"Yum," he smelled strawberries!

Matty was so excited about this adventure that he didn't notice the hole in front of him.

"Uh Oh," Matty cried out,

landing on something soft and furry.

"PORTOS"

"Woof , Woof", cried the white furry creature.

When Matty saw what he had landed on,

a rush of happiness bubbled up inside of him.

"Portos!" he yelled excitedly.

"Hello, young Matty," Portos greeted him enthusiastically,
"What are you doing down here?"

Matty blurted out, "The better question is,
Portos. What are YOU doing down here?"

"I'm counting these little dots on the strawberries I've found,"
explained Portos cheerily.

"That is a strange thing to do," Matty said.
"But I like it"

"You can help me if you want" Portos said.

After a while of counting the seeds of the strawberries (and eating them),

Portos looked at his small helper and gently said,

"You know, Matty, we all are a different in our own ways. look at me counting the dots on strawberries, sometimes it's difficult to see the world differently, but You are You, and isn't that something to be proud of?"

Matty sighed, **"But what about my wings?** I wish I could fit in, and I dream about flying like my family and the other kids."

"Oh, Matty, we all have dreams of what we want to be, that's just normal, but first we have to appreciate who we are," said Portos in a calming way.

"**Woooof,** when I was younger, Matty, like you,

I also thought I wasn't enough."

"Until I realized one day that differences are not only normal but they are important, like my counting the seeds on the strawberries.

But, I HATED being different it **until**…

"Until I began to understand myself."

CHAPTER FIVE /AN ADVENTURE WITH PORTOS

"But Portos, Matty protested,

what is normal or important about these questions:

That I can't fly?

That I can't see the clouds?

That I never know what to say to the other kids?

That somehow everyone I meet thinks I'm weird?

That I love finding interesting images on leaves?"

"Let me help you, Matty,

I want to show you something," said Portos.

"Come with me"

They ran into a part of the forest where Matty had never been.

To his surprise, the first thing Matty noticed was the countless leaves on the ground. Almost immediately, he began to see exciting images and shapes.

Portos said, "Come on and use your **wonderful weirdness and magical glasses** as your strength. Find two leaves with a sun and a moon.

Matty didn't need to be told twice. He eagerly began to scan each leaf. Soon, he found an impressive sun and a mystical moon.

"Wow," Portos gasped. "They are perfect."

"What do you need them for?" Matty asked curiously.

"We have to help a dear friend of mine." responded Portos.

Portos grabbed the leaves and cried out
"Come with me Matty,"as he
jumped onto a wooden box
on a thick rope, hanging
from a giant oak tree.

Matty caught up, completely out
of breath. "Portos," he screamed,
as he looked at the bizarre sight.
"What is that crazy contraption
you are on?"

"What are you waiting for?" Portos yelled. "Hop on!"

Matty climbed on and felt the box shaking and moving. He saw the ground was getting more and more distant, and the crown of the oak was getting closer and closer.

"Wow, Portos, I'M FLYING!"

"Yes Matty, you are at last flying, like in your dreams.
Now you can see the leaves up close."

"AMAZING! This is how the others must feel when they are flying," shouted Matty.

Portos just smiled.

No wonder the others liked going to school, they could fly on incredible adventures through fluffy clouds. They soared over treetops, while he crawled along the ground. Matty felt happy he could fly, but sad that he didn't have wings.

Portos commanded,

"Hold on Matty. We're now entering the **Leaves Sphere.**"

Matty couldn't believe his eyes as the wooden box carried him higher and higher into the air.

The wind rushed past his ears, and he held onto the box and Portos's fur.

He was excited and nervous. His heart was racing as he saw the big bushes below shrink to miniature plants. The rabbits disappeared out of sight.

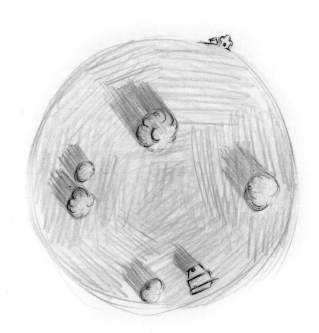

Matty suddenly screamed.

"Portos, I'm scared,

where are we going ?"

Portos laughed.

"Matty, we are going to a special place, where my best friend lives."

The wonderful flying box
stopped in front of a
charming treehouse, nestled
cozily into the branches of
the giant oak tree.

Matty's eyes sparkled.

"What is this place?" he asked.

Never in his young life had he seen such a building. All the buildings he had known were grey, cold stone caves constructed by bat architects.

But this was something else. It looked so warm and welcoming, so colorful and happy - exactly how he would build a home.

"It's the coolest treehouse you'll ever visit!" Portos answered, "I have plenty of amazing memories here" he smiled.

"Matty, with you, there are many more to come."

CHAPTER SIX/MEET LUNA

They jumped out of the box, walked to the door and knocked.

"Who is it?"

They heard a high-pitched voice from within.

The door swung open. Matty's eyes almost fell out of his head.

Never in his life had he seen such a majestic creature.

A dark gray, slim and elegant being with shimmering eyes and a
smiling mouth with big sharp teeth greeted them.

"If it isn't Portos, my bestest of best friends!" the creature whispered excitedly before she jumped and hugged him tightly.

"Luna, this is young Matty. I am sure you'll like him!" Portos said.

Luna walked up to Matty, who, at that point, couldn't stop staring into her mesmerizing eyes.

He stammered "He…He..llo," and swallowed every other word forming on his tongue.

"Hi Matty, it's a pleasure to meet you, won't you come in and join me for tea?"

Matty stood in the middle of Luna's living room, his eyes drawn to the framed phot**os** on the walls.   Some pictures of Luna with Portos, but Luna mostly with **Owls.**

Matty just stared and didn't know what to do.

Luna approached him with a warm smile, "Ah, as I see, you're exploring my memories," she said sweetly.

"Luna, why are so many big birds in your pictures?" Matty asked shyly.

"That's my family. I know I don't look like it, but my parents and brothers are **owls,"** she said. Luna's eyes seemed full of love as she now remembered those precious moments.

"I grew up with them and went to a famous owls' school in a castle. I had many struggles throughout my childhood. It was a challenging time. I had to learn many things."

It was so incredible. Imagine a cat raised by a family of owls – such a thing was almost too hard to believe.

To Matty's total surprise, Luna put on a pair of beautiful magical glasses and said "growing up with a family of owls wasn't like 'tea and cookies.'

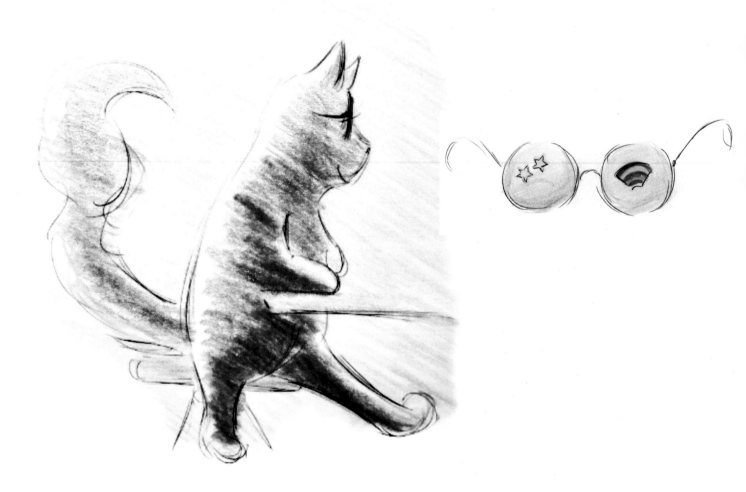

When I was young, I was so shy I didn't even want to talk to anyone, but when someone finally mentioned my interests, I couldn't stop talking.
I wasn't that popular in Owls Elementary School, or especially Owls High."

But listen, Matty, eventually I met an owl with magical glasses, we became very, very close friends!"

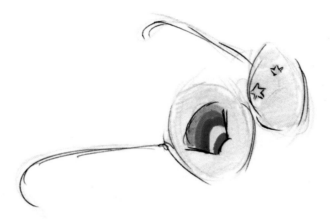

Luna went on, "Matty, through those experiences at home and in school, I learned how the world without magical glasses works. I made new friends. They understood me, and loved hearing about what I could see."

 Matty was captivated. He could listen to Luna all day

"I've learned so much, Matty.

I learned how to blend my glasses into me.

And Matty, I can teach you how to do that."

They talked and talked

Matty realized how comfortable he felt with Luna and Portos. It was remarkable – they barely knew each other, but he felt so understood.

He wished that Sira and Lira could see him right now, so chatty and happy. He was never like that with them or at school.

Wasn't it unbelievable what Luna had said about her childhood? How she struggled? She was truly the coolest being he had ever met.

He suddenly remembered why they had come to visit Luna in the first place..

THE LEAVES

CHAPTER SEVEN / THE MEANING OF LEAVES

"Luna, I want to show you something", said Matty

Surprised, she watched him rummage through his little bag. His fingers were shaking. He was nervous and excited to show her.

He showed her the leaves.   He   saw her yellow eyes brighten even more, like a night sky full of twinkling stars.

"This is exactly what I've been looking for, "Oh Matty, how did you know?"

Luna stared at her newest treasures and smiled from cheek to cheek.

"Come with me. Matty, I have something to show you."

The Hall of Leaves

Luna guided Matty and Portos through a hallway covered
with the most beautiful leaves Matty had ever seen. He really
wanted to stop and look, but Luna urged, "Come, Come."

They arrived at a room far beyond anything Matty had ever imagined. The colors, shapes, smells were overwhelming.

He stared in awe.   Each leaf he saw had something unique on it.

He spotted owls, cats, ice cream cones, a castle, and a huge friendly-looking bear.

Looking closer, he realized that all the leaves, like a tapestry, seemed to tell a story.

"Wow, what is this?"
Exclaimed Matty.

Luna told Matty that all those leaves told the story of her life.

Matty noticed on one particular leaf.

A sad Luna with her glasses on.

She was crying, surrounded by young

owl classmates laughing at her.

Luna explained how she tried to fit in, but the owls always flew away. Even worse, the mean owls mocked her for her hobby of collecting interesting leaves.

Luna continued

"We all have our stories and pains. I am sure everyone of us has felt lonely at one point.

But when we realize that we are not alone, and there are owls, bats, mice, dogs and cats who understand each other. Then it feels like a sunny summer afternoon with chocolate ice cream."

"Do you know what I mean?"

Portos spoke up

"I remember back in my day (a hundred or so years ago) that the other dogs in my class treated me differently," Portos said.

"Did they call you names? "
Asked Matty.

Portos continued, "No, they ignored me most of the time," he sighed, "and I could never really understand why."

"What's the solution?" Matty asked.

The Wisdom of Luna and Portos

"Well, there is no universal solution," Luna revealed.

"Our motto is: stay strong, respect and love yourself, and know that you're good the way you are. Life is a learning experience and a journey."

Portos added, "We can use our magical glasses to see the world both ways. Our way and how others see us."

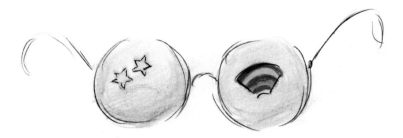

Portos continued, "Matty, you're allowed to ask for help, There are many who will understand you and your magical glasses."

"They might even become close friends."

CHAPTER EIGHT/THE SURPRISE AT SCHOOL

What a memorable day for Matty!

On his way back home, running with Portos, he felt fantastic. Finally, someone understood him. He felt spring in his step and hope in his heart.

Tomorrow was school.

Portos agreed to take him to the bats school. Matty was not scared for the first time in forever. Actually, he was excited because he wanted to look for bats with magical glasses.

Who knew? Maybe there was a friend waiting for him he had never even noticed before? Maybe he could show one or two mean classmates what it is like to see with magical glasses.

But, Matty cautioned himself, one thing at a time.

But, one thing at a time

When Matty got to school he instantly noticed a new classmate, a cool little girl. He was shocked, she wore big beautiful magical glasses. The others quickly began to find her weird. Those glasses?!

After school, Matty ran to find Luna and Portros.

"Luna, there was a new little girl in school today. She wore magical glasses, just like you told me!!" Matty stated in an animated way.

"Yes, Matty, look at her eyes, closely. She had magical glasses, just like the ones on your nose, my invisible ones, and the ones Portos hides behind his fluffy eyes," Luna explained.

"Wow!" Matty was excited. A girl with magical glasses? He wondered if there were others with magical glasses in his bat school.

The next day

Matty hurried to the bat school cave. He carefully checked some of the other kids' faces. There were bats with hats, and bats with braces, but no bats with magical glasses.

But then

He noticed a girl walking into the next-door classroom. He swore he saw colorful glasses on her nose. He wanted to follow her, but the class bell rang.

Matty was so excited he couldn't concentrate on the equations and numbers that piled up on the chalkboard in front of him. All he thought about was how to find that mysterious girl

After school

Matty went back into the bat school and searched every cave, looked everywhere, went outside, checked every pond, every small bush in the schoolyard, but there was no trace of her.

Where was the girl with the magical glasses?

He started to think that maybe his imagination had played a trick on him.

But Matty knew what he had seen.

Matty needed to see Portos and Luna

He rode the wooden box to the treehouse.

"I'm soooooo frustrated," Matty said,

as they sat down for tea. Matty told them about the girl with the colorful, magical glasses and how he couldn't find her.

"Hmm, that is very interesting, Matty," said Luna. "I don't think that your mind has played a trick on you."

"Maybe she's just excellent at masking?" Portos pondered.

"What in the world of bats and cats is masking?" Matty asked.

Luna explained, "some who see and think like we do, may try to copy or pretend to do things the way others do. It's like wearing a mask to fit in with the others."

"They can do that?" Matty was puzzled.

"Yes, that's something that those wearing magical glasses do a lot," Portos said. "And some of them have an amazing talent for acting in theaters because of that."

Portos scratched his nose. "Do you have a theater club in bats school?"

"That might be it!" said Matty. "We have a musical theatre show coming up, and the students are practicing every free minute!"

The next morning

Matty's parents were surprised when he left the house much earlier and much happier than usual.

Matty wanted to find out where the theatre club was before recess began. He knew that they were practicing during recess.

Matty found he right place, the sign said **Class 1B**. He could tell by the stage and lights. Yes, this is where they rehearse.

And There She Was

CHAPTER NINE / MAKING A FRIEND

And there she was

the mysterious girl, rehearsing everyday, except this time she wasn't wearing colorful magical glasses.

But then he realized why. She was on stage, performing like the best actress he had ever seen. He was stunned when he realized that she was the leading character of "The Fly Warrior".

He watched the play until they were finished.

Then he took a big, the biggest breath he had ever taken, and said,

"Hey, I'm Matty. I loved your acting. What's your name?"

"I'm Yara, wait, let me..." She grabbed her colorful glasses and put them on. And looked at Matty and grinned.

Matty felt happy. They walked and talked for a while and Yara told him all about the theatre club and the upcoming play. Matty loved to listen and he bravely asked if she wanted to have tea. She was popular. The mean kids were becoming friendly, because she was the star actor, even though she was wearing those huge magical glasses.

Yara was a riddle to him.

Tea With Yara

Yara looked right at him,

"You want to ask why I'm popular even though I'm one of these," she tapped on her glasses. "How did you know what I wanted to ask?" he was confused. **"Do you have superpowers?"**

"Maybe a little," Yara said and grinned. "I was aware of the fact that I'm different from others when I was super young. And so, I began to study their behavior very early on and thought lots about what they felt in many different situations."

"Wow," Matty was puzzled. She was an expert in living with magical glasses.

Yara continued, "I became better and better at understanding other people, so I could put on masks for different situations which sparked my interest in acting, and then I don't need to wear glasses."

"Now, Matty, I'm just me. With my glasses, and I wish I knew more people like us."

It was beginning to make sense

Portos and Luna were right about the masking.
Matty was speechless.

Yara was awesome. Matty had to invite her to
the treehouse to meet Portos and Luna.

Yara nodded "yes" and soon they were rushing
together through the forest to the big oak tree.

Like one big family

Portos and Luna welcomed Yara warmly into their arms.
Matty was so proud of them and his new friend Yara.
He could not stop smiling the whole time.

Yara told Luna and Portos all about the theatre club.
Luna and Portos told delightful stories from their lives.
Matty sat there with a warm feeling of belonging.

They made plans to throw a magical glasses
party after the big theatre performance !

The day had finally arrived

"The Fly Warrior", starring Yara. Oh what a brilliant performance, "Bravo, Bravo". Yara received a standing ovation.

Then there was the after party

They all celebrated! Rabbits, hedgehogs, mice, dogs, cats, bats, rats, owls, and even two frogs from faraway Frog-Town. The wonderful thing was that some guests wore magical glasses, some didn't.

What fun it was!

Matty's parents now understood his magical glasses. They were so proud of him, even Sira and Lira apologized for their behavior. Some of the Matty's mean classmates, seeing him with Yara, gave him a respectful nod and smile.

The weeks went by

Matty was happier than ever before. Every day in recess, he watched Yara's theatre practice. After school, they flew (with him on her back) to the treehouse.

Joyful times

CHAPTER TEN/FRIENDS WITHOUT ENDS

Matty, Luna, Portos, and Yara gathered at the treehouse,
the stars twinkled above.

Matty spoke to each of them from his happy heart.

"Portos, you were the first person to show me true friendship. You taught me that I'm allowed to get help. And you helped me. Thank you so much."

"Oh, Luna, your motto -- be strong, love yourself, know you are good the way you are -- that will be be my motto too. I'm forever grateful."

"And Yara, when we had tea, you shared your life story with me, I learned to listen and to understand, and how to fit in with my magical glasses."

And Life Was Good

Hey, readers of my book. Please Come to our THANK YOU PARTY

"Hello, Hello,

My giant human friends,

we are here because

we want to say

Thank you!"

"Thank you, Irena, for writing my story, it was a joy working with you!

And, a big thanks to Ruben and his incredible drawing talent that has given me and my friends our wonderful smiles and fur and glasses!

Rod and Mark, without you, it would have been chaos, thank you, creative team, for your tireless efforts in putting this book together – Thank you!